A celebration of Autumn in rhyme

Mariana Books
Rhyming Series
Book 3 Seasons

By
Roger Carlson

When August fades into September,
and you start to feel a nip in the air;
it can only mean one thing:
autumn is nearly there!

1

The sunny days of summer
slowly begin to let go.
The leaves on the trees change color,
and start to fall to the ground below.

The weather gets colder,
and the temperatures drop.
Farmers work hard to harvest
their favorite autumn crop.

Green turns to yellow,
orange, brown, and red.
Scattered leaves line every street,
garden, yard, and shed.

5

Rosy red apples
ready for that first bite.
Fields full of yellow corn
glisten in the sunlight.

Huge orange pumpkins
creeping along the ground;
are collected and kept aside
for when Halloween comes around.

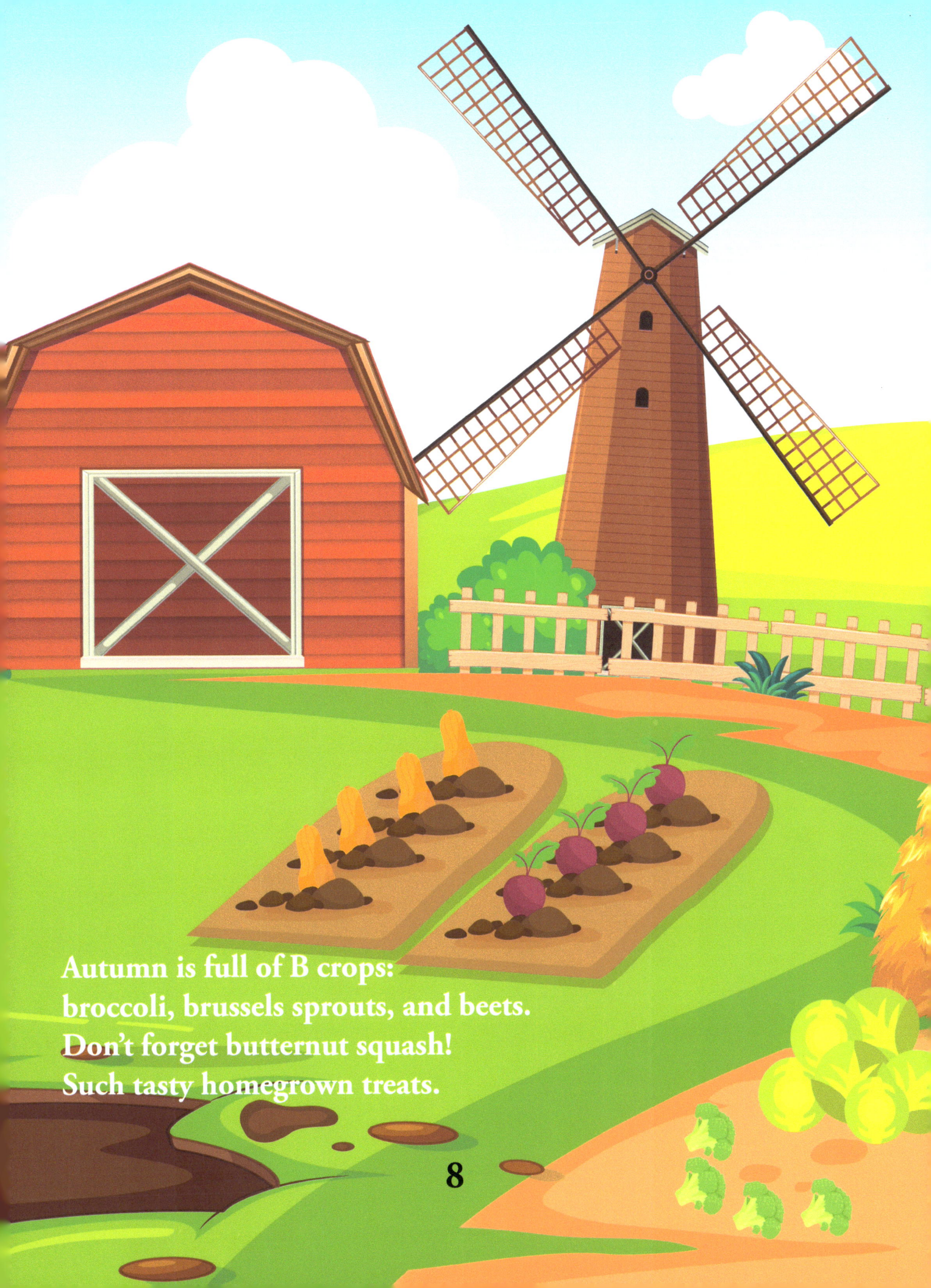

Autumn is full of B crops:
broccoli, brussels sprouts, and beets.
Don't forget butternut squash!
Such tasty homegrown treats.

It's not just plants and food
that go through change.
Everyone starts wearing hats
and warm scarves in a wide range.

The chilly weather increases
with every passing date.
Some animals start gathering food
to fill their winter plate.

Plump chipmunks and bushy-tailed squirrels
look with their eyes bright and wide;
they gather nuts, acorns, and berries,
then store them safe inside.

Big burly bears with shaggy fur
prepare for winter's fate.
They find cozy caves to keep them safe
while they hibernate.

Box turtles of every size,
whether they're big or small,
curl up inside their shells
to sleep throughout it all.

Then, there's the garter snake
snoozing in his den.
He won't disturb you when it's cold,
but once it's warm, he'll be back again.

14

And here's the prickly hedgehog
in her nest between these logs.
She'll sleep the whole winter long
unless she's bothered by someone's dogs.

And oh, the birds in autumn
all ages, young or old;
they spread their wings and soar away
when the weather first gets cold.

If you look up, you might see geese
flying in a V-shape.
They're on their way south
for a warm winter escape.

But it's not just the geese
seeking a warmer place;
for several other birds,
it's the same case.

Sweet swallows, merry martins,
turtle doves and even wrens
leave their summer nests behind,
and fly south with all their friends.

So we know the leaves will fall,
and must be piled in a heap.
Many birds will fly away,
while animals curl up to sleep.

Sometimes it feels like life stands still
while waiting for the spring.
So some might dread the start of autumn;
but wait, there's one more thing!

COLLEGE

21

Autumn starts an important season,
I think you know what I mean.
The holiday season, when we celebrate with family,
which starts with Halloween!

People carve their pumpkins,
and light them up at night.
Glowing eyes and crooked smiles,
might give you quite a fright!

And oh, the Halloween decorations,
you'll see them all around.
They're in the yard, on the house,
even on the ground.

Kids make ghost costumes from sheets,
and cut circles out for eyes.
Kids meet up for trick-or-treat
all dressed up in disguise.

25

You'll see mummies and skeletons,
fairies, witches, and cats.
Wizards waving magic wands
while wearing wizard hats.

HAPPY HALLOWEEN

R.I.P

HALLOWEEN PARTY

Go to a haunted house and you will find
a scare in every room.
If you're lucky, you might see
a witch flying on her broom.

27

Kids dress up as anything they want to be,
and then they walk the streets.
During trick-or-treating time,
kids get lots of candy treats!

After Halloween is through,
there's no more spooky pranks.
Then it's time to gather around
with loved ones to give thanks.

For friends, for family,
for all the good out there;
Thanksgiving is the time,
to give thanks and share.

The family table is full of food
to fill our plates and bowls;
Thanksgiving always smells so good
especially the rolls.

A giant turkey is the main dish,
with mashed potatoes and candied yams;
cranberry sauce, green beans, and
rolls with homemade jams.

There's thick, hot gravy
and stuffing you just can't beat;
roasted veggies straight from the oven,
and tons of desserts to eat!

So when the weather's turning cold,
and it's beginning to look like autumn,
enjoy the autumn season,
and absorb the wonder of it all!

34

So enjoy the autumn season,
wrap yourself up well;
for the cold season will be upon us,
and soon, it'll be time for Noel!

Find these and all of the other Mariana Publishing books for sale on Amazon and our web site
www.marianapublishing.com

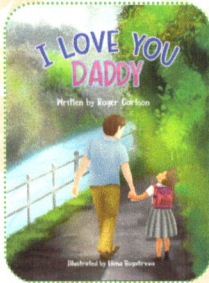

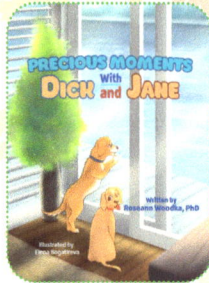

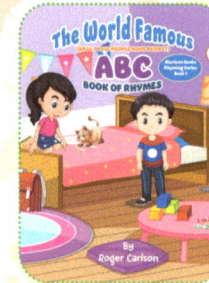

WAYBACK BOOKS

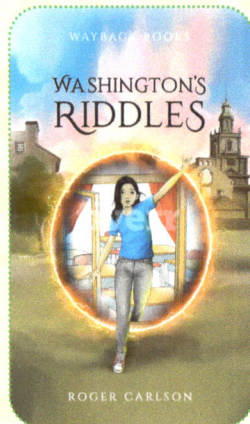

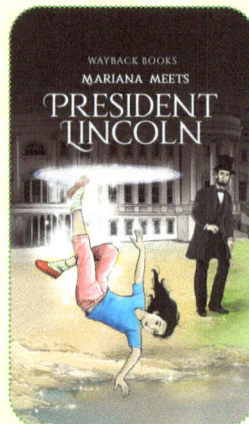

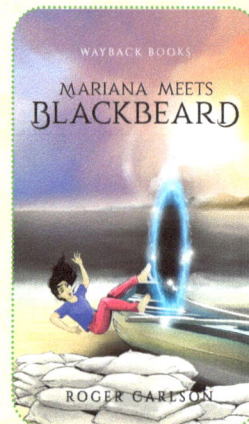

Find us on:

f @marianapublishing   @marianapublishing   @LlcMariana   Mariana Publishing Online

ISBN: 978-1-64510-042-3 (Hardback)
ISBN: 978-1-64510-041-6 (Amazon Paperback)
ISBN: 978-1-64510-043-0 (Print On Demand)